A GIFT FOR:

Pat

FROM:

Jodi

DATE:

February 14, 2005

Crazy About MY Husband

BARBOUR
PUBLISHING

CRAZY ABOUT MY HUSBAND™

COPYRIGHT © 2002 BY MARK GILROY COMMUNICATIONS, INC.
TULSA, OKLAHOMA

ART AND DESIGN BY JACKSON DESIGN COMPANY
SILOAM SPRINGS, ARKANSAS

ISBN 1-59310-279-8

SCRIPTURE QUOTATIONS MARKED NLT ARE TAKEN FROM *THE HOLY BIBLE, NEW LIVING TRANSLATION*,
COPYRIGHT © 1996. USED BY PERMISSION OF TYNDALE HOUSE PUBLISHERS, INC., WHEATON,
ILLINOIS 60189. ALL RIGHTS RESERVED.

PUBLISHED BY BARBOUR PUBLISHING, INC., P.O. BOX 719, UHRICHSVILLE, OHIO 44683,
www.barbourbooks.com

Member of the
Evangelical Christian
Publishers Association

PRINTED IN CHINA.

Crazy About Love

LOVE IS PATIENT AND KIND. LOVE IS NOT
JEALOUS OR BOASTFUL OR PROUD OR RUDE.
LOVE DOES NOT DEMAND ITS OWN WAY. LOVE IS
NOT IRRITABLE, AND IT KEEPS NO RECORD OF
WHEN IT HAS BEEN WRONGED. IT IS NEVER GLAD
ABOUT INJUSTICE BUT REJOICES WHENEVER THE
TRUTH WINS OUT. LOVE NEVER GIVES UP, NEVER
LOSES FAITH, IS ALWAYS HOPEFUL, AND
ENDURES THROUGH EVERY CIRCUMSTANCE.
LOVE WILL LAST FOREVER.

1 CORINTHIANS 13:4-8, NLT

I'M CRAZY ABOUT MY HUSBAND
BECAUSE HE'S GIFTED
IN THE CULINARY ARTS.

(AS LONG AS I KEEP HIM OUTSIDE.)

Even when you start adding spices to dishes I'm preparing without asking.

you're gifted inside too!

I'M CRAZY ABOUT MY HUSBAND
BECAUSE HE STILL OPENS THE
CAR DOOR FOR ME.

(ALTHOUGH HE DOESN'T ALWAYS STICK
AROUND TO SHUT IT ANYMORE.)

At least when my hands are full or I'm dropping things

I'M CRAZY ABOUT MY HUSBAND
BECAUSE HE'S GOT INITIATIVE.

(HE BELIEVES THE EARLY BIRD GETS THE WORM.)

I'M CRAZY ABOUT MY HUSBAND
BECAUSE HE'S A JOY TO SLEEP ^(NAKED) WITH!

You don't push me away when I want to cuddle!

I'M CRAZY ABOUT MY HUSBAND
AND LOVE TO SPEND A SATURDAY
AFTERNOON IN AUGUST IN THE
BACK YARD WITH HIM.

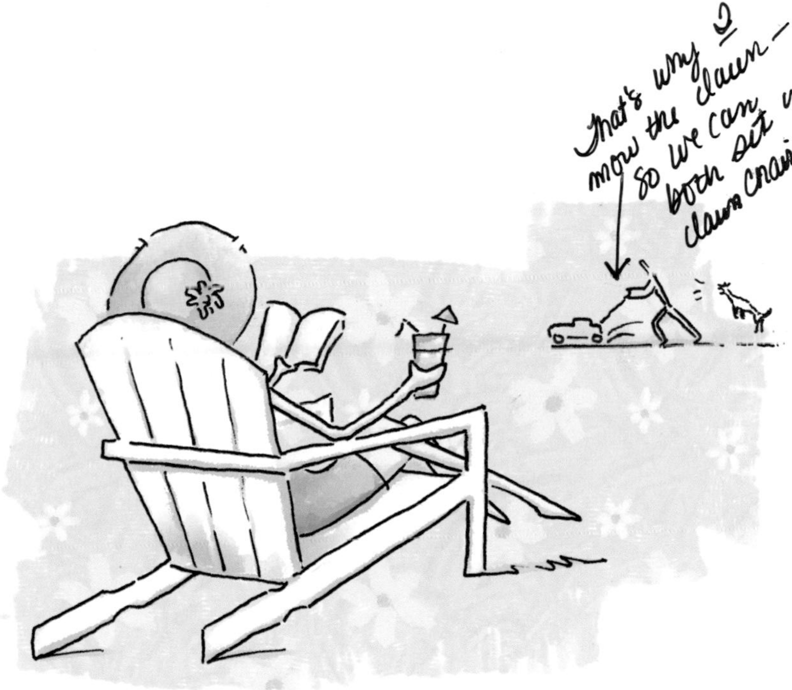
That's why I
mow the lawn—
so we can
both sit in
lawn chairs!!

No dear, I don't think that new dress makes you look heavy. In fact, I think it makes you look thinner.

I'M CRAZY ABOUT MY HUSBAND
BECAUSE HE IS ALWAYS HONEST.

(AND WISE.)

*Thank you
for the
emeny compliments.*

I'M CRAZY ABOUT MY HUSBAND
BECAUSE HE GETS LOTS OF EXERCISE
AND STAYS IN GOOD SHAPE.

(HE TOLD ME HE'S GOING OUT FOR A WALK TODAY.)

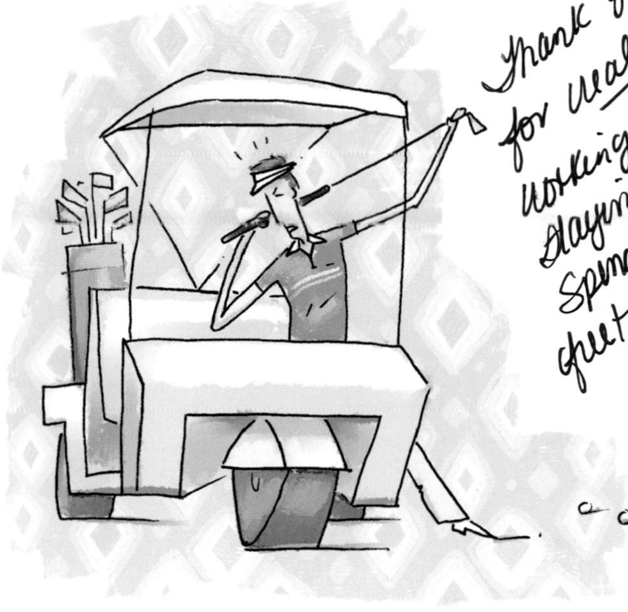

I'M CRAZY ABOUT MY HUSBAND

BECAUSE HE KNOWS WHEN

AND HOW TO BE TOUGH. — *well– not when Payton's touching your TV!*

(I'M ALSO GLAD WE PUT OUR BIG SCREEN IN THE ~~BASEMENT!~~ *Family Room*)

I'M CRAZY ABOUT MY HUSBAND
BECAUSE HE'S FAITHFUL AND TRUE,
AND HE ONLY HAS EYES FOR ME.

(ALTHOUGH I DO HELP HIM AVOID TEMPTATION AT THE MALL!)

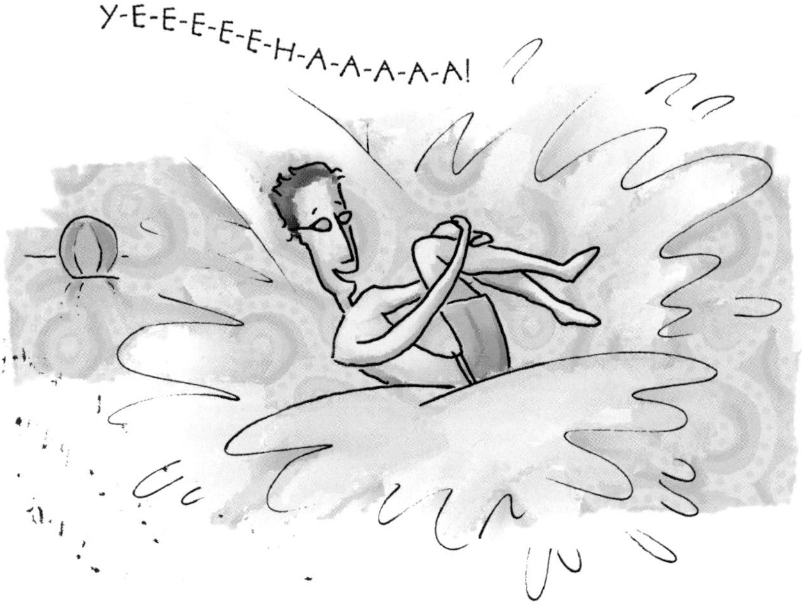
Y-E-E-E-E-E-H-A-A-A-A-A!

I'M CRAZY ABOUT MY HUSBAND
BECAUSE HE IS STILL A BOY AT HEART!

(AND I REALLY DON'T MIND A **FEW** WRINKLES
AND GRAY HAIRS TO GO ALONG WITH MINE!)

Thank you for being
a Your dad & great
husband!

I'M CRAZY ABOUT MY HUSBAND
BECAUSE HE'S MAN ENOUGH TO EXPRESS
HIS FEELINGS AND EMOTIONS.

A-A-A-A-A-A-A-A-A-A-A-R-G-H!
Thank You
for not using
bad language (too often!)

Thank you for making sure my naked body is covered!

I'M CRAZY ABOUT MY HUSBAND
BECAUSE HE ALWAYS
SHARES THE COVERS.

(EXCEPT ON SOME OF THE COLD NIGHTS.)

I'M CRAZY ABOUT MY HUSBAND
BECAUSE HE GETS
INTO THE HOLIDAY SPIRIT.

Thank you for always checking the lights & putting the 13 ft. tree up & standing up on the top rung of the ladder to do it.

you are so beau-u-u-u-u-u-u-tiful, to me-e-e-e-e!

Thank you for sharing special songs w/ me!

I'M CRAZY ABOUT MY HUSBAND
BECAUSE HE SINGS BEAUTIFUL
LOVE SONGS TO ME.

I'M CRAZY ABOUT MY HUSBAND
BECAUSE HE CAN WHIP UP A
QUICK MEAL WHEN I'M TOO
TIRED TO COOK.

Dinner's ready-y-y-y-y!

Thank you for bring home GFS meals!

I'M CRAZY ABOUT MY HUSBAND
BECAUSE HE CAN FIX JUST ABOUT
ANYTHING THAT'S BROKEN.

You have become very handy the last 13 years!

I'M CRAZY ABOUT MY HUSBAND
BECAUSE HE DRESSES FOR SUCCESS.

GO TIGERS!

#1

You never complain about the clothes I choose for you!

I'M CRAZY ABOUT MY HUSBAND
BECAUSE OF HIS WITTY SENSE
OF HUMOR—HE STILL KNOWS
HOW TO MAKE ME LAUGH!

Or laugh at me!

Thank you for being you—for to be w1!

I'M CRAZY ABOUT MY HUSBAND
BECAUSE HE KNOWS JUST WHAT TO DO
WHEN I FEEL SAD AND START CRYING.

Unless I'm crying because of you!

Honey, I'm taking the kids to the park!

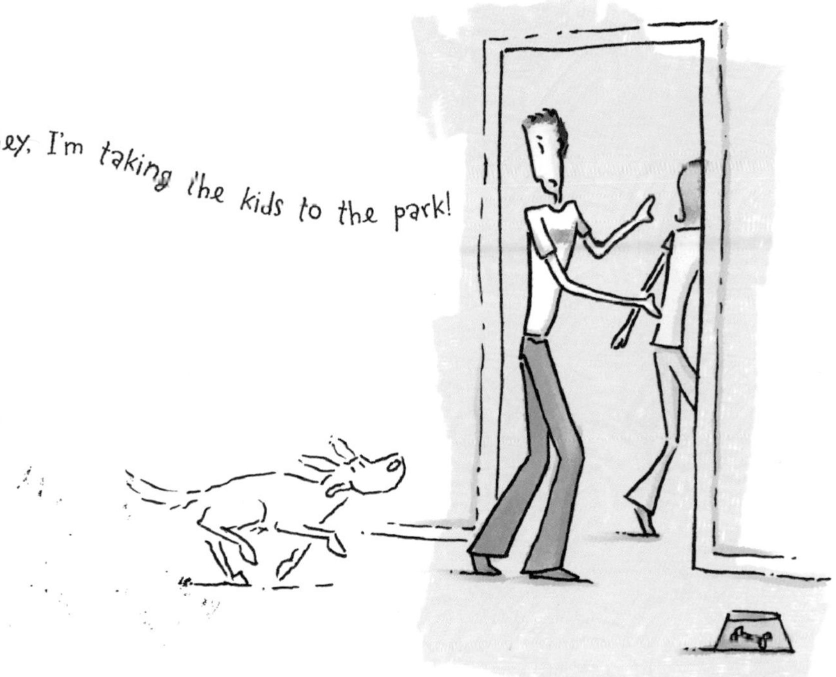

I'M CRAZY ABOUT MY HUSBAND
BECAUSE HE'S NEVER LOST HIS
LOVE OF LEARNING.

(HE LOVES TO SPEND TIME IN HIS OWN SPECIAL LIBRARY.)

Way too true!

I'M CRAZY ABOUT MY HUSBAND
BECAUSE HE KNOWS HOW
TO HANDLE THOSE AGGRESSIVE
DOOR-TO-DOOR SALESMEN.

Thanks, Mister . . . that's a record!

Well @ least you bought 3 boxes of Girl Scout Cookies. That's splurging for you!

I'M CRAZY ABOUT MY HUSBAND
BECAUSE HE'S THE MOST PATIENT
MAN IN THE WORLD WHEN WE SHOP.

You really are !! :)

I'M CRAZY ABOUT MY HUSBAND
BECAUSE HE'S HAPPY TO BE
SETTLED DOWN.

So you're SURE you can deliver those
flowers within the next hour?

I'M CRAZY ABOUT MY HUSBAND
BECAUSE HE ALWAYS
REMEMBERS SPECIAL OCCASIONS,
LIKE OUR ANNIVERSARY.

You do! — At least w/ help of your palm pilot!

Thank you

I'M CRAZY ABOUT MY
HUSBAND BECAUSE HE'S
AN INCURABLE ROMANTIC.

(UNTIL ABOUT 10:05.)

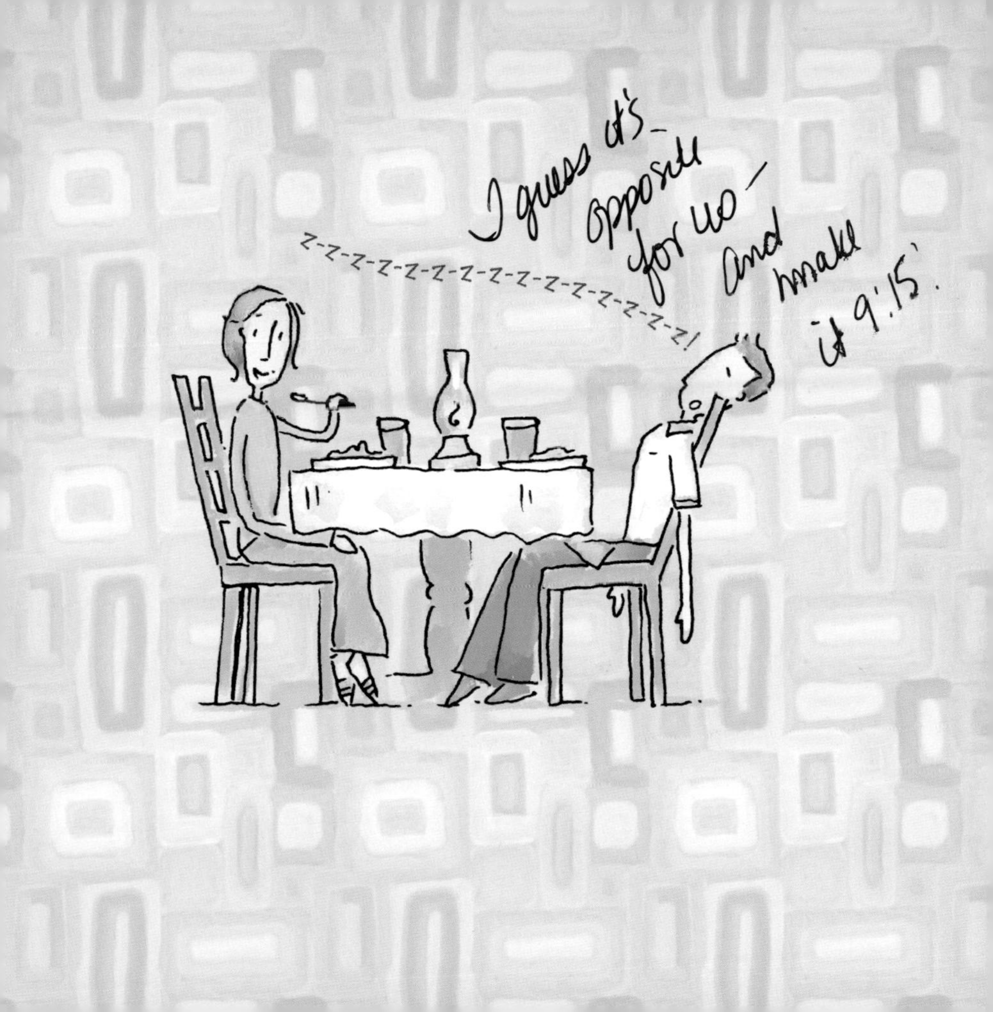

z-z-z-z-z-z-z-z-z-z-z-z-z-z-z!
I guess it's— opposite for us— And make it 9:15.

I'M CRAZY ABOUT MY HUSBAND
BECAUSE OF HIS SELF-CONFIDENCE
AND QUIET DETERMINATION.

Pool pump -
Garbage disposal
Hot tub filter ...
You've really
come a long
way!

I'M CRAZY ABOUT MY HUSBAND
BECAUSE WE LOVE WATCHING
MOVIES TOGETHER.

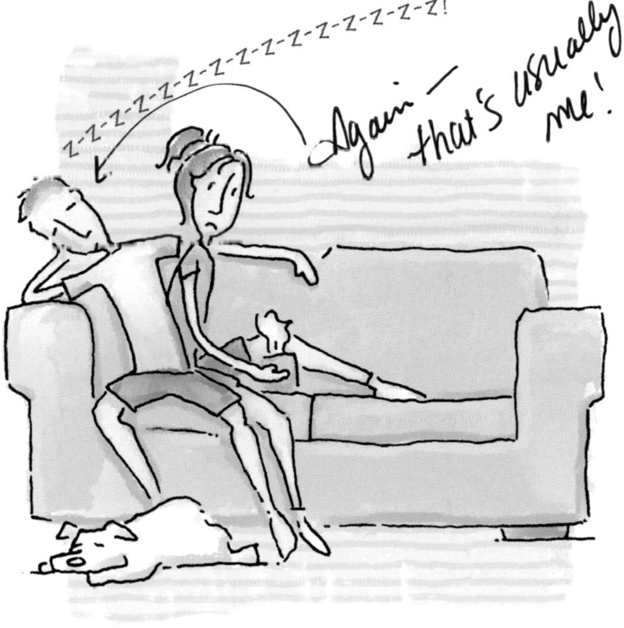
Z-Z-Z-Z-Z-Z-Z-Z-Z-Z-Z-Z-Z-Z-Z-Z-Z-Z!
Again — that's usually me!

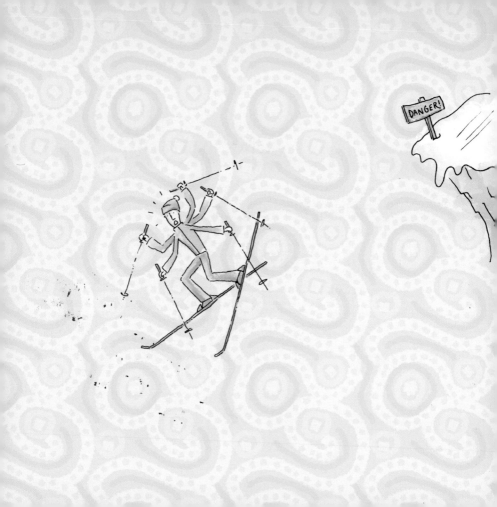

I'M CRAZY ABOUT MY HUSBAND
BECAUSE OF HIS GO-FOR-IT
PERSONALITY.

Well, you did try the Rockin' Roller Coaster @ Mom!

I'M CRAZY ABOUT MY
HUSBAND BECAUSE HE IS ONE
UNBELIEVABLE KISSER!

(AND HIS HUGS AREN'T TOO BAD EITHER.)

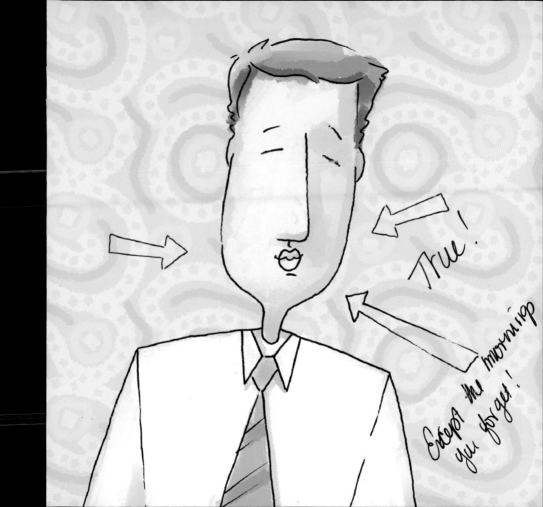

You want me to wear THAT on Valentine's Day?!

I'M CRAZY ABOUT MY HUSBAND
BECAUSE HE STILL FINDS ME
VERY ATTRACTIVE.

You do choose nice lingerie!

I'M CRAZY ABOUT MY HUSBAND
BECAUSE HE STILL GETS EXCITED
WHEN HE HEARS "OUR SONG."

I'M CRAZY ABOUT MY HUSBAND
BECAUSE HE DOESN'T DO
THINGS HALFWAY.

You don't & just train,
you bag too!

I'M CRAZY ABOUT MY HUSBAND
BECAUSE HE ALWAYS KNOWS
JUST WHAT TO BUY FOR ME.

I'M CRAZY ABOUT MY
HUSBAND BECAUSE HE BRINGS
HOME THE BACON!

(I JUST WISH HE'D LEAVE SOME OF
THE OTHER STUFF AT THE STORE.)

You do usually
add more
to the cart then
the kids do!

I'M CRAZY ABOUT MY HUSBAND
BECAUSE HE LOOKS LIKE A
MILLION BUCKS ON DATE NIGHT.

(EVEN IF WE ARE USING A BUY ONE,
GET ONE FREE COUPON FOR DINNER!)

Trub

I'M CRAZY ABOUT MY HUSBAND
BECAUSE HE KNOWS THAT SOMETIMES
YOU HAVE TO ASK FOR DIRECTIONS.

Well - you don't ask for
road directions but you
are good @ seeking
direction from God
through prayer.

Thank you!

I'M CRAZY ABOUT MY HUSBAND
BECAUSE HE CAN BE COUNTED ON
TO DO THE RIGHT THING.

(EVEN WHEN HE DOESN'T HAVE TO.)

I'M CRAZY ABOUT MY HUSBAND
BECAUSE HE KNOWS HOW TO
MAKE A BAD DAY SUDDENLY BETTER.

true!! :)

I'M CRAZY ABOUT MY HUSBAND
BECAUSE HE IS ALWAYS READY
TO TAKE CARE OF THE LITTLE
THINGS IN LIFE.

And they all lived happily ever after.

Thank you for
Sharing your
time W/
W0!

Chicken no-o-o-o-dle!

I'M CRAZY ABOUT MY HUSBAND
BECAUSE HE'S COMMITTED TO
ME IN SICKNESS AND IN HEALTH.

You have always taken good care of me!

I'M CRAZY ABOUT MY HUSBAND
BECAUSE HE STILL GETS
MY HEART RACING.

I'M CRAZY ABOUT MY HUSBAND
BECAUSE HE MAKES ME FEEL
SAFE AND PROTECTED.

You do 🙂

I'M CRAZY ABOUT MY HUSBAND
BECAUSE HE WILL GO
THE EXTRA MILE FOR ME.

I'M CRAZY ABOUT MY HUSBAND
BECAUSE I STILL BELIEVE
HE IS A GIFT FROM GOD.

You are :. I thank
God for such an
incredible gift!

I'M CRAZY ABOUT MY HUSBAND
BECAUSE HE'S STILL
CRAZY ABOUT ME!

I'M CRAZY ABOUT MY HUSBAND BECAUSE HE'S STILL THE ONLY MAN FOR ME!

EVERY TIME I THINK OF YOU, I GIVE THANKS TO MY GOD. I ALWAYS PRAY FOR YOU, AND I MAKE MY REQUESTS WITH A HEART FULL OF JOY.

PHILIPPIANS 1:3-4, NLT